Dear Future Spouse

Reflections

Alasha Bennett

DMU Publishing
Virginia Beach, VA

Dating Mechanics LLC.
Virginia Beach, VA. www.DMU.solutions

Written by Alasha Bennett.
Cover designed by Lee Dear Jr.

ISBN: 978-0-9986275-1-9

Printed in the United States of America

Contents

How to use the reflection book

This reflection book works with the Dear Future Spouse Journal. Each day's journal writing can be recorded in this book for easy referencing. Included are additional exercises based on the original reflection pages. It is beneficial for you to do the reflections because they require ACTION! Connecting with your future spouse starts with you taking the steps to prepare a space for them in your life. This journal will help you do that.

Day 1

Preparation

Dear Future Spouse......

_____

_____

_____

_____

_____

_____

Dear Future Spouse

_____

_____

_____

_____

_____

_____

_____

_____

_____

_____

_____

_____

_____

_____

_____

_____

Dear Future Spouse

_____

_____

_____

_____

_____

_____

_____

_____

_____

_____

_____

_____

_____

_____

Dear Future Spouse

Reflection

Take one action and plan how you will accomplish it. What are the steps you need to take to be successful? Add as many steps as needed.

Action: _____

Start Date: _____

Step one: _____

Step two: _____

Step three: _____

Step four: _____

Step five: _____

Step six: _____

Step seven: _____

Day 2

Worth the Wait

Dear Future Spouse……

_____

_____

_____

_____

_____

_____

Dear Future Spouse

_____

_____

_____

_____

_____

_____

_____

_____

_____

_____

_____

_____

_____

_____

_____

_____

Dear Future Spouse

_____

_____

_____

_____

_____

_____

_____

_____

_____

_____

_____

_____

_____

_____

_____

Reflection

You must live every day to the fullest before you meet your spouse and after. How will you spend your time as you wait for your spouse to enter your life?

_____

_____

_____

_____

_____

_____

_____

_____

_____

_____

Day 3

Resolve in Love

Dear Future Spouse….

_____

_____

_____

_____

_____

_____

_____

Dear Future Spouse

_____

_____

_____

_____

_____

_____

_____

_____

_____

_____

_____

_____

_____

_____

_____

Dear Future Spouse

_____

_____

_____

_____

_____

_____

_____

_____

_____

_____

_____

_____

_____

_____

Reflection

From the negative reactions circled, how do you feel about your actions after the situations is over? How does the person feel who is on the receiving end of those actions? How will you incorporate some of the positive ways of dealing with conflict?

_____

_____

_____

_____

_____

_____

_____

_____

_____

_____

Day 4

Cooking from the Heart

Dear Future Spouse......

_____

_____

_____

_____

_____

_____

Dear Future Spouse

_____

_____

_____

_____

_____

_____

_____

_____

_____

_____

_____

_____

_____

_____

_____

_____

Dear Future Spouse

_____

_____

_____

_____

_____

_____

_____

_____

_____

_____

_____

_____

_____

Reflection

Write a list of characteristics you want in your future spouse.

Which of these characteristics do you currently exhibit and which ones do you need to improve on?

_____

_____

_____

_____

_____

_____

_____

_____

_____

Day 5

My Biggest Fear

Dear Future Spouse……

_____

_____

_____

_____

_____

_____

Dear Future Spouse

_____

_____

_____

_____

_____

_____

_____

_____

_____

_____

_____

_____

_____

_____

_____

_____

Dear Future Spouse

_____

_____

_____

_____

_____

_____

_____

_____

_____

_____

_____

_____

_____

_____

Dear Future Spouse

Reflection

How to change your belief about marriage and release the fear.

__Step one__: Acknowledging the belief.
Example: Say it out loud or write it down. (You did this in your journal entry.)

__Step two:__ Understanding this is simply your viewpoint from experience but does not hold truth for every person. Seek out a situation that makes your belief false.
Example: You believe all marriages eventually end in divorce. Find a widower or an elderly person who was married for over 20 years without divorcing.

__Step three:__ Create a new belief.
Example: Every marriage does not end in divorce.

__Step four:__ Act with the new belief in mind.
Example: Speak life into your future marriage by changing your words to reflect the new belief. "My marriage will be successful and will not end in divorce. We will be happily married for many years."

Dear Future Spouse

Step one: What is your belief?

_____

_____

Step two: What situation did you use to make your belief false?

_____

_____

_____

_____

_____

_____

_____

_____

_____

Step three: Create a new belief by stating the exact opposite of the old belief.

_____

Step four: Write a positive affirmation that incorporates the new belief using personal pronouns such as I, we, us, me.

_____

_____

Day 6

Sweet Words of Love

Dear Future Spouse……

_____

_____

_____

_____

_____

_____

_____

Dear Future Spouse

Dear Future Spouse

_____

_____

_____

_____

_____

_____

_____

_____

_____

_____

_____

_____

_____

_____

Reflection

There is more to attraction beside physical features. What causes a person to be sexy in your eyes?

_____

_____

_____

_____

_____

_____

_____

_____

_____

_____

Day 7

Selfless Acts

Dear Future Spouse……

_____

_____

_____

_____

_____

_____

_____

Dear Future Spouse

Dear Future Spouse

_____

_____

_____

_____

_____

_____

_____

_____

_____

_____

_____

_____

_____

Reflection

Do something for someone else anonymously. Write it here but only share it with your spouse.

Day 8

We're Meant to Win

Dear Future Spouse……

_____

_____

_____

_____

_____

_____

_____

Dear Future Spouse

Dear Future Spouse

Reflection

Teams celebrate their success as they should. A marriage anniversary is cause for jubilation. What would be a nice celebration for your first anniversary?

_____

_____

_____

_____

_____

_____

_____

_____

_____

Day 9

My Romantic Side

Dear Future Spouse......

_____

_____

_____

_____

_____

_____

Dear Future Spouse

_____

_____

_____

_____

_____

_____

_____

_____

_____

_____

_____

_____

_____

_____

Dear Future Spouse

Dear Future Spouse

Reflection

Is there a fantasy you've had that you would like to try? Are there things that you wouldn't consider doing?

_____

_____

_____

_____

_____

_____

_____

_____

_____

_____

_____

Day 10

Our Financial Future

Dear Future Spouse……

_____

_____

_____

_____

_____

_____

Dear Future Spouse

Dear Future Spouse

_____

_____

_____

_____

_____

_____

_____

_____

_____

_____

_____

_____

_____

_____

_____

Reflection

How would you like the finances to be handled? Would you like one joint account, separate accounts or a combination of both?

_____

_____

_____

_____

_____

_____

_____

_____

_____

_____

_____

Day 11

Love in the Spirit

Dear Future Spouse……

_____

_____

_____

_____

_____

_____

_____

Dear Future Spouse

_____

_____

_____

_____

_____

_____

_____

_____

_____

_____

_____

_____

_____

_____

_____

Dear Future Spouse

_____

_____

_____

_____

_____

_____

_____

_____

_____

_____

_____

_____

_____

_____

_____

_____

Reflection

Where would you like to grow over the next year in your spiritual walk?

_____

_____

_____

_____

_____

_____

_____

_____

_____

_____

_____

_____

Day 12

Purpose and Plan

Dear Future Spouse……

_____

_____

_____

_____

_____

_____

Dear Future Spouse

Dear Future Spouse

_____

_____

_____

_____

_____

_____

_____

_____

_____

_____

_____

_____

_____

_____

Reflection

What would you do for the pure joy you would get from it? There would be no compensation of any kind in return.

_____

_____

_____

_____

_____

_____

_____

_____

_____

_____

Day 13

Building our Family Together

Dear Future Spouse……

_____

_____

_____

_____

_____

_____

Dear Future Spouse

Dear Future Spouse

Reflection

Name the people in your life that your spouse should recognize as holding a special place in your heart.

_____

_____

_____

_____

_____

_____

_____

_____

_____

_____

Day 14

Refresh, Renew, Rejuvenate

Dear Future Spouse……

_____

_____

_____

_____

_____

_____

_____

Dear Future Spouse

_____

_____

_____

_____

_____

_____

_____

_____

_____

_____

_____

_____

_____

_____

Dear Future Spouse

_____

_____

_____

_____

_____

_____

_____

_____

_____

_____

_____

_____

_____

_____

_____

Reflection

Apprecaition is one way someone can feel restored. How can your spouse show their appreciation for you?

_____

_____

_____

_____

_____

_____

_____

_____

_____

_____

((Day 15))

My Heart in Your Hands

Dear Future Spouse……

_____

_____

_____

_____

_____

_____

Dear Future Spouse

_____

_____

_____

_____

_____

_____

_____

_____

_____

_____

_____

_____

_____

Dear Future Spouse

_____

_____

_____

_____

_____

_____

_____

_____

_____

_____

_____

_____

_____

_____

Dear Future Spouse

Reflection

What actions do you contribute to a person being untrustworthy?

_____

_____

_____

_____

_____

_____

_____

_____

_____

_____

(Day 16)

Music Therapy

Dear Future Spouse......

_____

_____

_____

_____

_____

_____

Dear Future Spouse

Dear Future Spouse

_____

_____

_____

_____

_____

_____

_____

_____

_____

_____

_____

_____

_____

_____

Reflection

Make a wedding playlist to share with your future spouse. Rotate the songs into your current playlist or create a CD you can listen to.

Day 17

Healthy for my Love

Dear Future Spouse……

_____

_____

_____

_____

_____

_____

Dear Future Spouse

_____

_____

_____

_____

_____

_____

_____

_____

_____

_____

_____

_____

_____

_____

_____

_____

Dear Future Spouse

_____

_____

_____

_____

_____

_____

_____

_____

_____

_____

_____

_____

_____

Reflection

What things will you do to keep the fire burning bright in your marriage? Research things couples do to keep the fire burning in their marriage. Which ones are you willing to try?

_____

_____

_____

_____

_____

_____

_____

_____

_____

_____

Day 18

Making Decisions Together

Dear Future Spouse……

_____

_____

_____

_____

_____

_____

Dear Future Spouse

Dear Future Spouse

Dear Future Spouse

Reflection

Draft a step by step plan to share with your spouse for making decisions concerning at least one of these issues.

-Spending money on items outside of the agreed budget.
-A spouses unhealthy or destructive habits or behaviors.
-Disciplining the children.
-Pets in the home.
-Lack of bonding time, sexual or intimate satisfaction.
-Achieving personal goals.
-Heated disagreements.
-A spouse feeling underappreciated or unloved.

_____

_____

_____

_____

_____

_____

Dear Future Spouse

_____

_____

_____

_____

_____

_____

_____

_____

_____

_____

_____

_____

_____

_____

Dear Future Spouse

_____

_____

_____

_____

_____

_____

_____

_____

_____

_____

_____

_____

_____

_____

Day 19

Committed for Life

Dear Future Spouse……

_____

_____

_____

_____

_____

_____

Dear Future Spouse

Dear Future Spouse

_____

_____

_____

_____

_____

_____

_____

_____

_____

_____

_____

_____

_____

_____

_____

Reflection

List some expectations you have for marriage. Talk with a few married people about your expectations. Are they realistic for a marriage? If not, are you willing to change those expectations?

_____

_____

_____

_____

_____

_____

_____

_____

_____

_____

Day 20

Bound by Love

Dear Future Spouse……

_____

_____

_____

_____

_____

_____

Dear Future Spouse

Dear Future Spouse

_____

_____

_____

_____

_____

_____

_____

_____

_____

_____

_____

_____

_____

_____

Reflection

Take one boundary you don't want your spouse to overstep and explain the reason why you have that boundary?

Day 21

Speaking Love into Existence

Dear Future Spouse......

_____

_____

_____

_____

_____

_____

Dear Future Spouse

_____

_____

_____

_____

_____

_____

_____

_____

_____

_____

_____

_____

_____

_____

Dear Future Spouse

Reflection

What do you plan to change that will cause your spouse to feel invited and welcome?

_____

_____

_____

_____

_____

_____

_____

_____

_____

_____

Day 22

Changed by Love

Dear Future Spouse……

_____

_____

_____

_____

_____

_____

Dear Future Spouse

Dear Future Spouse

_____

_____

_____

_____

_____

_____

_____

_____

_____

_____

_____

_____

_____

_____

_____

_____

Reflection

What specific habit will you change or be mindful of as you prepare for your spouse?

_____

_____

_____

_____

_____

_____

_____

_____

_____

_____

_____

Day 23

Happy Ever After

Dear Future Spouse......

_____

_____

_____

_____

_____

_____

Dear Future Spouse

Dear Future Spouse

Reflection

What about the character's actions is like how you would react? What about the character's actions is different than how you would react?

Day 24

Emotional Triggers

Dear Future Spouse....

_____

_____

_____

_____

_____

_____

Dear Future Spouse

_____

_____

_____

_____

_____

_____

_____

_____

_____

_____

_____

_____

_____

Dear Future Spouse

_____

_____

_____

_____

_____

_____

_____

_____

_____

_____

_____

_____

_____

_____

_____

Reflection

What is one specific triggers you are willing to work on understanding and resolving to have a better marriage?

_____

_____

_____

_____

_____

_____

_____

_____

Day 25

Love Transformation

Dear Future Spouse……

_____

_____

_____

_____

_____

_____

Dear Future Spouse

_____

_____

_____

_____

_____

_____

_____

_____

_____

_____

_____

_____

_____

_____

Dear Future Spouse

_____

_____

_____

_____

_____

_____

_____

_____

_____

_____

_____

_____

_____

_____

Dear Future Spouse

Reflection

What traits are you ready to develop or strengthen through the love your partner shows?

_____

_____

_____

_____

_____

_____

_____

_____

_____

_____

Day 26

Marriage Goals

Dear Future Spouse......

_____

_____

_____

_____

_____

_____

Dear Future Spouse

_____

_____

_____

_____

_____

_____

_____

_____

_____

_____

_____

_____

_____

_____

Dear Future Spouse

_____

_____

_____

_____

_____

_____

_____

_____

_____

_____

_____

_____

_____

_____

Reflection

What will people know about you from how your spouse treats you?

_____

_____

_____

_____

_____

_____

_____

_____

_____

_____

Day 27

Love as Motivation

Dear Future Spouse......

_____

_____

_____

_____

_____

_____

Dear Future Spouse

Dear Future Spouse

_____

_____

_____

_____

_____

_____

_____

_____

_____

_____

_____

_____

_____

_____

Reflection

How confident are you that love is possible for you?

_____

_____

_____

_____

_____

_____

_____

_____

_____

_____

Day 28

Fulfilling the Vows

Dear Future Spouse……

_____

_____

_____

_____

_____

_____

Dear Future Spouse

Dear Future Spouse

_____

_____

_____

_____

_____

_____

_____

_____

_____

_____

_____

_____

_____

_____

_____

_____

_____

Dear Future Spouse

Reflection

What promises would you like to include in your vows?

_____

_____

_____

_____

_____

_____

_____

_____

_____

_____

(Day 29)

My Partners Happiness

Dear Future Spouse……

_____

_____

_____

_____

_____

_____

Dear Future Spouse

Dear Future Spouse

_____

_____

_____

_____

_____

_____

_____

_____

_____

_____

_____

_____

_____

_____

_____

_____

Dear Future Spouse

Reflection

What impact will you make on your partner's life by speaking life into them?

_____

_____

_____

_____

_____

_____

_____

_____

_____

_____

Day 30

In Love we Grow

Dear Future Spouse……

_____

_____

_____

_____

_____

_____

Dear Future Spouse

Dear Future Spouse

_____

_____

_____

_____

_____

_____

_____

_____

_____

_____

_____

_____

Dear Future Spouse

Reflection

Congratulations! You have come to the last day of your journal. Are you clearer now than before you started about your personal reasons for wanting to be married and what being in a union with your most trusted friend will be like? It was my pleasure to guide you through these 30 days and encourage you to keep moving forward on the road to finding the right person for you.

Often people start on the path to love but get distracted. What I want is for you to reach your goal. You may feel like giving up, like happiness is far away. Know that your diligence in preparing for your spouse will be rewarded. You have planted your intentions now you must continue to water it so that your intentions grow into something tangible.

Your next step on your journey to love is to learn how to date with purpose. Visit Dating Mechanics University at www.dmu.solutions to get more information on how to stay on the path to true love.

Dear Future Spouse

**Improve your dating and relationship skills by
taking a course online at
Dating Mechanics University**

Avoiding the Pitfalls of Love

The Relationship Readiness Quiz

The Relationship Readiness Assessment

Dating for Success

Single Parent Quiz

Understanding Your Value

How to Figure Men Out

Building Successful Relationships

Dear Future Spouse

Books from the DMU library.

Dear Future Spouse
7 Key Questions to Ask Before a First Date
Attract the Right Man for You
The First Date Checklist
Dating Mechanics

About the Author

Alasha Bennett is a Relationship and Dating Coach and Founder of Dating Mechanics University. Her workshops, dating clinics and seminars focus on helping singles become aware of their dating habits and styles so they can be successful in finding a partner. She encourages singles to take the theory of dating and put it into practice so they can realize their dream of true love.

www.ingramcontent.com/pod-product-compliance
Lightning Source LLC
Chambersburg PA
CBHW061736020426
42331CB00006B/1258